20 Effective Tips to Overcome Stress

Stop Worrying and Start Living

Jamie Botello

© 2015

Table of Contents

Chapter 7

Connect with OthersConclusion

Conclusion

responsibility of the recipient reader. Under no circumstances will any legal responsibility or blame be held against the publisher for any reparation, damages, or monetary loss due to the information herein, either directly or indirectly.

Respective authors own all copyrights not held by the publisher.

The information herein is offered for informational purposes solely, and is universal as so. The presentation of the information is without contract or any type of guarantee assurance.

The trademarks that are used are without any consent, and the publication of the trademark is without permission or backing by the trademark owner. All trademarks and brands within this book are for clarifying purposes only and are owned by the owners themselves, not affiliated with this document.

Introduction

When things don't work out as you had planned and careen out of your control, being stressed and anxious is a natural outcome. An urgent crisis at work or home that you need to address immediately is bound to create stress in you. You feel nauseous, your head may hurt, or you are just overwhelmed.

However, at moments of crisis you need to be of a mind that is free of stress, so you can solve the problem satisfactorily. It is vital to overcome the stress as it is part of living a healthy life just as you need proper exercise and diet. Since stress is not something, you can just wish away, you need to know how to manage it.

Further, stress can affect each and every part of your personal and professional life. To maintain good emotional and physical health, you should know how to tackle stress and deal with it effectively.

Life is precious and spending your time stressed out and anxious, is not the way to live it. Finding a way to overcome the stress will benefit you immensely. This eBook aims at targeting the causes of stress and the ways by which stress can be removed successfully from your life, so you can stop worrying and start living your life joyfully and contentedly.

Chapter 1

Overview of Stress

Stress is a very common word in the urban dictionary. Most of the world population today deals with stress in one form or the other; be it less or more. We say that we are in stress when we strongly feel that the situation is beyond our control and we doubt our capabilities to cope with it. The overload of pressure or emotions becomes too much for us to handle.

How stress is good?

Contrary to the common perception, stress is not always bad. There is a good kind of stress as well, which gets us going. This good stress keeps many people active and gives a necessary push to them when necessary. For example, when students have exams, they just forget everything else. All they want is to study. The motivation from teachers or parents and the stress of competition with the fellow students encourages them to study harder. They are rewarded when they perform well. The same stress becomes bad when the parents threaten them to top the class, else they will be punished. At such times, the bad stress takes its toll on their performance and sometimes, on their life.

There is a very fine line between good stress and bad stress. When this line is crossed, people become depressed or their health deteriorates. In this book, we will discuss about the bad stress and how to deal with it.

There are two terms, when we talk about stress- "stress" and "stressor". Stress is that feeling of anxiety when are under pressure. Stressor is the factor, due to which, stress is caused. We respond to stressors and come under stress. For example, unpleasant people, loud noise, the nervousness before a presentation, etc. are the examples of stressors.

Chapter 2

Ill Effects of Stress

Stress has many negative symptoms on body and mind. Often, mental stress leads to physical illness or some other visible symptoms. Mental stress is generally not noticed by other people. Hence, it is neglected too. But, it is crucial that the symptoms are taken seriously and steps are taken as soon as possible to cure it.

Mental symptoms of stress are:

- Restlessness
- Anxiety
- Lack of focus and motivation
- Anger or irritability
- Depression or unhappiness in general

Physical symptoms of stress are:

- Pains or aches in different body parts
- Constipation or diarrhea

- Dizziness or nausea
- Rapid heartbeat or chest pain
- Frequent cold
- Lack of sex drive

Behavioral symptoms of stress are:

- Eating too much or too less

Sleeping too little or too much

- Isolation from others
- Procrastinating responsibilities
- Use of cigarettes, alcohol or drugs for relaxation
- Nail biting or pacing, etc.- nervous habits

Cognitive symptoms of stress are:

- Weak memory
- Lack of concentration
- Poor judgment
- Being pessimistic
- Constantly worrying about something
- Racing thoughts

It is important to note that it is not necessary that if you are experiencing any of the above symptoms, you are under stress. Sometimes, these symptoms are caused due to other medical problems as well. Consult a doctor to ascertain your correct situation. There are several common reasons for people to feel stressed. Some of them are:

External causes:

- Major changes in life
- Negative environment at school or office
- Relationship difficulties
- Being extremely busy in life
- Financial problems
- Responsibilities of family

Internal causes:

- Excessive worrying
- Pessimism
- Unrealistic expectations
- Pessimistic self-talk
- Rigidity in life, inflexible attitude
- Attitude of "all or nothing"

Chapter 3

Diet and Exercises

You must have heard many tips for overcoming stress. People often tend to cure their mental problems themselves. However, this is not the correct method. You must either consult a doctor or refer to the correct sources to cure your stress. Here, we have listed 20 authentic methods of overcoming stress. Go through them and incorporate them in your daily routine, whichever method suits you best.

1. Diet for Stress Relief

Yes, there are some foods, which can actually relieve you from stress. These foods help you to stabilize your blood sugar, and improve the emotional response of your mind. You can look up to these foods when you have had just enough:

- **Leafy Green Vegetables**: It is always tempting to lay your hands on a cheese pizza when you are stressed. But, go green is the new mantra for kicking off stress. You

8

will feel calmer and more energetic when you consume veggies.

- **Turkey breast:** This amazing food is full of proteins. And foods that contain proteins help to produce serotonin, which regulates your happiness and hunger. Thus, you can completely rely on turkey breast and other protein-rich foods when you feel stressed.

- **Oatmeal:** We know that you feel like feeding yourself with lots of carbohydrates when you are stressed. We do not recommend suppressing all your cravings. Instead, reach for complex carbohydrates like oatmeal, which does not raise your blood sugar.

- **Yogurt:** Though it needs more research to prove the benefits of yogurt as anti-stress food. But the protein and calcium, in addition to probiotics in yoghurt, is definitely good for relieving stress.

- **Salmon fish:** This variety of fish is high in protein, omega-3 fatty acids and Vitamin D. the anti-inflammatory properties of salmon let you relax from the adverse effects of hormonal stress.

A quick overview of many other such foods are: pistachios, blueberries, dark chocolate, fortified milk, pumpkin seeds, flax seeds sunflower seeds, avocado, cashews, etc.

2.   Foods to Avoid

While there are many foods that help you elevate your mood, there are many that will stoop down your anxiety levels even more. Strangely, our body craves for such foods only during stress. But, you should strictly avoid some foods, which are a complete "no" while are you feeling low.

Energy drinks: You may think that drinks like coffee, caffeinated colas and other energy drinks might uplift your mood. But, caffeine and sugar are worst foods for stress. Avoid them completely.

Spicy food: These foods take longer to digest. Thus, foods that contain lots of spices may aggravate your discomfort.

Sweets and Candies: They increase your craving to eat more and more. Plus, they contain sugar, which we have already mentioned, is not good for body anyhow, when taken in excess.

Alcohol: It is a huge misconception that alcohol brings down the stress. But, it is not true. In fact, it stimulates the production of Cortisol, which is a steroid hormone, and increases blood sugar and decreases formation of bones.

Coffee: When you feel agitated in office or at home, you would make the matter worse by reaching for a sugary coffee. As already mentioned above, its caffeine may increase your stress level.

Processed foods: We all love those colorful packets of chips and biscuits. But, control your cravings for processed foods during stress because the salt and sugar in these foods also increases your Cortisol levels.

Sugar-free candies and gums: They do not contribute to stress directly but they can exaggerate digestive issues related to stress and thus make you even more uncomfortable.

3. Sleep for Better Stress Management

Sleep is one such gift of God, when taken in right amount, can take you up to high levels of health and wealth. But, considering the modern lifestyle, we often tend to sacrifice their sleep only. Sometimes, we do so intentionally and many a times unintentionally. We are often worried about the activities of the day and instead of shutting down our mind at night, we race up our thoughts even more. Taking less sleep affects our immune system.

Quality of sleep: Stress often messes up your quality of sleep. And you turn and toss whole night when you feel anxious just before you sleep. It may make you insomniac in long term. Try not to think about negative thoughts when you go to bed. Think positive thoughts and slowly reduce the amount of thoughts. You will experience much better quality of sleep.

Avoid the vicious cycle: When you do not take proper sleep, you feel dizzy throughout the next day. This, in turn, affects your efficiency and you take even more stress. And, this cycle goes on forever. If you feel that you need to correct your cycle of sleep, take a day off and bring your sleeping cycle back to the right track.

Smell some floral scent: Smelling floral scents like lavender just before sleeping relaxes your body and induces deep sleep.

Relaxation technique: You can also try some techniques like meditation, yoga and progressive relaxation before you log off to bed.

Deep breathing: Long inhaling and exhaling breaths naturally calms down your body and leads you to dreamland.

4. Exercises for Stress

You are already aware that exercising can radically improve your health. But, it is a lesser known fact that exercise is also tremendously good for your mental health as well. Let us quickly go through the benefits of exercise for relieving stress:

- Endorphins levels are pumped up when you take a good running. Endorphin is a neurotransmitter which makes you feel good.

- When you take up a vigorous exercise like swimming or

a tennis round, you will notice that you did not think about the tensions of your life for a single second. Your mind automatically focuses on such activities. Induce such activities in your routine and you will notice change in your personality in just a few days.

- Exercising daily boosts your self-confidence. And you bring up a positive outlook towards life when you feel good about yourself.

- Exercise also makes your body positively tired and induces good sleep.

How to start exercising?

Read below to find out what suits you best.

Build up the exercise regime gradually: You can start brisk walking first and then take it up to running a few hours a week. 150 minutes of moderate exercise and 75 minutes of vigorous exercise is recommended for an average individual.

Take up what you enjoy: You should always incorporate such exercises in your routine, which you enjoy. If you do not enjoy it, you will not be able to follow the routine forever. You can start with anything like stair climbing, swimming, weight lifting, gardening, jogging, bicycling, jogging, etc.

5. Hobbies to Get Rid of Stress

It is always beneficial to cope with stress when you have some hobbies to spend your time well. You might have noticed that when you enjoy doing something, you almost lose the track of time. This is the theory behind counting hobbies as stress busters. Hobbies are always good for feeling good, energized and relaxed.

You can choose a hobby which makes you feel successful. You will notice that your sense of wellbeing and self-esteem will increase tremendously. Here is a list of some helpful activities which can help you ward off stress from your mind.

Listening to music and singing

Music is the food for soul. Keep some of your favorite songs in your mobile and listen to them whenever you feel low. You can also plug in your headphones and sing out loud your favorite song. Do not hesitate and try it. You will feel heavenly.

You can also learn to play a new musical instrument like guitar, violin or piano. It gives a new form of self-esteem.

Reading

Books are the best friends of humans. You must have already heard of that. Pick up your favorite book and indulge yourself in the pages. Utilize your free time; you spend chronically worrying about the unworthy facts of your life, in reading. Body muscles relax a lot when you just lie down and concentrate on reading.

Writing

Just take up a pen and a paper; write down your exact feelings when you feel worried or stressed and burn it off. It will remove your worries completely. You never know, eventually, you might discover a new writer in you.

Scrapbooking

Rather than doing it alone, call your friends and relatives to dinner and scrapbook your photos and memories. You will thank yourself for doing this. Creative things like these are a great stress buster.

Cooking

Even if you do not know cooking, it is a great art to learn and forget all your worries. You can also find a partner and learn delicious cuisines or just some brownies. Give yourself a feast and just be happy.

Chapter 4

Take Control

6.   Organize your Life

A clutter free life is what we always desire. Be it on an emotional level or on the physical plane in our homes, we always want a mess free life. But, very few of us dare to throw the problem-creating things and emotions out of our life. Here, we will talk about the clutter in your house and life, how it creates troubles for you and how to organize your life.

You have to throw many things out of you house so that you do not waste your time organizing them. You need to spend your valuable time doing your favorite activities and also spend it with your loved ones.

- Make a list of **top 5 priorities** in your life. Now note down where you waste your time and eliminate those activities completely.

- **Redesign your routine.** Yes, note down how you

spend your day. If you are not satisfied with your routine, you need to redesign it according to the things you love to do.

- **Learn to refuse.** You should refuse to people for not doing things they asked you to do. You must have surrendered many a times to others' wishes but now you need to change. It might make you feel guilty initially but eventually, you will realize that many people just "use" people who cannot say "no" for anything.

- **Limit the communication time.** It has become very easy these days to surrender to the necessary evils of internet and mobile these days. You just need to set a limit to respond to emails, text messages, calls, etc. and take out time for yourself

- **De-clutter your home.** You do not realize it many a times but there is a lot of stuff in your house that you do not use at all. Start eliminating with big things like furniture, gadgets, etc. that you no longer use. It is many times overwhelming to discard such big things but when they get out of your sight, you feel much more relaxed with the added breathing space.

- Now, come to **discard the smaller things**. Go to every room and make a list of all the things that you have not used in the past one year. Be brave and throw all those things out. It is even better if you donate them to the needy.

7. What you Should Avoid

There are many things in our life that make our lives stressful. You need to identify these things and avoid them completely to live a stress free life.

Identify the stressors: Make a list of top 10 stressful factors of your life and eliminate them. If it is not possible, try different ways to make them less stressful for you.

Avoid unnecessary commitments: You must be having commitments towards friends, family, kids, office, civic responsibilities, religious works, side work, online activities and many more. Evaluate your commitments and avoid the ones which cause the most stress for you. You do not need to be omnipresent for everyone.

Avoid procrastination: We all have a habit of piling up tasks. These tasks turn into a mountain and give unnecessary stress to us. Develop a habit of finishing all tasks within the deadline and you will realize you have turned your life positively upside down.

Avoid being late: You need to re-schedule your habits of your routine if you always get late to work, parties and other meetings. It becomes a habit without our realization and starts stressing us out. Ward off this unnecessary bad habit.

Avoid unnecessary expectations: We agree that you might be a perfectionist and you expect others also to perform at the same level. But, when they do not perform according to your expectations, you burn yourself of stress. Stop keeping unrealistic expectations from people and accept them the way they are. You will notice your relations becoming healthier with others and ultimately you will be the one who will be happier.

8.   Build your Defenses

Stress can make you ill. You might not take this fact seriously but it is a well-established fact that mental disturbances lead to physical illness. You need to build your defense against stress so that you do not fall prey to the side effects of stress. Emotions are directly related to your health. You must have noticed that when you feel low, your body also becomes lethargic. On the other hand, when you feel cheerful, you tend to perform better.

Chronic stress can lead to severe physical illnesses. Sometimes, you do not recognize stress, but it is there with you all the time. For example, if you have to take care of a severely sick person, you might come under stress. You may face stress due to work related problems, due to failure in relationships. Things like these are going to stay in one form or the other in your life. You just need to learn how to cope with them without taking much stress.

Just like we reboot our phone when it gets overworked, you need to recharge your body too. People these days pay more attention to gadgets and other things than on themselves. Appreciate your value and reboot yourself too whenever it is needed. We have already mentioned several methods to eliminate stress. Just give yourself the due importance and build up your defense mechanism against stress.

9. Learn To Monitor Stress Levels

Since stress symptoms affect your feelings, thoughts, behavior and entire body, you should know to recognize the stress symptoms easily, so you can manage them more effectively. When left untreated, stress leads to various health issues such as obesity, diabetes, heart disease, and high blood pressure.

The way people react to stressful situations, differ based on their specific personality and on the way they respond to pressure. One way to combat stress is to monitor your stress symptoms and the triggers, and try to reduce the triggers in your daily routine that bring on the stress.

Stress stems from routine activities without your realizing it and leaves behind lasting negative impact on your body, if not monitored and dealt with effectively. Therefore, it is important to monitor your stress levels continuously.

Chapter 5

Stop Worrying

10. Draw the Line Between Caring and Worrying

We all love and care for their friends and family. We never want to lose them. Caring is a part of loving. It means to provide to the family what they need for their health, wealth and protection. We always want to give to our family whatever they need. It is a form of positive energy. But, care is not always materialistic. It has a non-materialistic aspect as well. We have to be emotionally available for our family.

But, many a times, we forget that there is a difference between caring and worrying. Worrying is more like fearing the loss of someone or something. It can be specifically related to something and frighten a worried person. Else, it can be non-specific, which just creates anxiety in the habitually worried person. An anxious person is not sure what is bothering him, but he still worries constantly about random things. It is a form of negative energy.

Now, if we talk about relationships, you must have seen such people who just keep worrying about the safety of their loved ones. It is absolutely perfect to care for them. But eventually, they end up frustrating our loved ones if they show excess worry to their family. You need to understand the fine line between care and worry. We cannot control everything that is going on around us. Thus, even worrying about these things is not going to change them.

Worrying just causes stress. And you have to stay stress free to lead a happy life. To avoid this negative energy, you again need to focus on the positive aspect of everything. For example, you might worry that your teenage daughter has gone out with her friends for a late night party. Instead of worrying too much about her safety, you can explain to her your concerns and call her once in a while to affirm her safety. Constant nagging will frustrate her and she might become averse to your questions. There is a correct way to approach the problems. Try to see the right path and you will fell much less stressed.

11.   Face Challenges Head On

Sometimes, we get scared of new challenges in life and come

under stress even at the thought of them. Many a times, challenges are difficult to overcome. But, there is always a way out. Go through the guidelines mentioned below. They might help you to overcome stress caused by new challenges.

Focus on everything that is right: There are times when you think that you are broke. But, you need to shed some light on the things that are still in their place. They will help you to come out of the crises.

Take action: If the bigger picture intimidates you, focus on the smaller picture. Instead of thinking excessively about the big task in hand, break it into small parts day-wise. Accomplish your daily goals and you will achieve the whole task someday.

Embrace fear: You need to face your fears to eliminate them from your life. Do something every day that you are scared of. It can be as trivial as calling a long distance friend or speaking on a stage in front of public.

Do not give up: You might face obstacles and commit mistakes while facing your challenges. But, do not ever give up. Whenever you stumble, stand up and try again. You will thank yourself when you look back later.

12.   Embrace your Mistakes

- Human beings are created as a statue of mistakes. But, instead of accepting our mistakes, we tend to keep off them. This not only creates guilt for us, but also stresses our mind because we are not ready to learn from our mistakes when we do not accept them. We fear that we will be criticized for our errors and we do not want to face the shame. And, in the whole process, we sometimes make the same mistake again. Look at the following tips that might help you in embracing your own mistakes so that you can move ahead in life, stress free.

- **Forgive and let go:** You might think that you have committed a huge error and your family is never going to forgive you for that. But, you need to forgive yourself when you make a mistake. Then only, you can expect the world to forgive you. Mistakes are easier to correct if you stop punishing yourself for them.

- **Learn a lesson:** There are several mistakes you might

make and curse yourself for the same. But later, when you look at the bigger picture, you will realize that you needed to make that mistake to learn a valuable lesson. Many such errors prove to be a milestone in the long term.

- **Ask yourself the correct question:** Whenever you commit an error, instead of asking yourself the negative questions, you should ask yourself the positive ones. For instance, do not say, "Why do I make the same mistake every time?" You can ask yourself, "What should I do next time to avoid the same mistake?"

13.   Know your Limits

You need to know your limits of work and emotional level. Everyone is not made for every task. You do not need to always compare yourself with your fellow worker and have a low self-esteem just because he/ she has a high efficiency level. Just accept yourself the way you are. If you are not satisfied with yourself, you just need to work on your skills and learn time management.

Stop taking up new activities: You should complete the tasks in hand and only then you should take up any new activity. Just because a friend asked you to pick up her car from the mechanic because she is busy, you do not need to leave your priorities and say yes to her. Politely refuse and tell her the reasons. Sometimes, you might have to get diplomatic and make an excuse to her. But, it's okay once in a while. You do not need to take all the guilt plus stress.

Stop multi-tasking: You need to stop multi-tasking if it is affecting all your tasks at hand. If you are not able to manage two things at a time, you need to cut down on your list of tasks at hand.

Make a calendar: Make a single calendar or an organizer diary to mark all the tasks weekly. This will help you to remember all the things and cut down on avoidable tasks.

Chapter 6

Motivation

14.   Motivation is the Key

We have already talked about the positive stress and negative stress in the initial chapters. You know that positive stress can act as a motivator in your professional life. But, negative stress can take away all the motivation and hinder your performance. It is important to stay motivated during our extremely demanding lives. But often, we face those days when we feel lethargic and do not have any motivation to work. At such times, you need to find stimulants, which will motivate you back to your normal life.

There three simple ways to manage stress and maintain motivation:

• Positive thinking

• Setting achievable goals
  Have a good social support system

- We have already talked about positive thinking. So let us focus on the other two things.

- **Setting achievable goals:** You should not set such goals which are unrealistic for you. Rather, aim for such goals, which you think you can achieve easily. Gradually, you can aim for more. Keeping small goals in the beginning gives you a sense of accomplishment and you feel motivated to perform better. If you have your seniors who set your targets, you can ask them to assign you work according to your capabilities. If you explain to them in correct words (remember positive explanation), they will surely understand.

- **Social Support System:** It is important to maintain a social support system around you. It can be in the form of family, friends or colleagues. They are a great support in tough times. Whenever, you feel de-motivated, you can look up to them for encouragement. They may give you some effective ways to cope with the stressors of your life.

15. Positive Mindset

It is crucial to maintain a positive mindset to attain the lowest possible stress level. Though the modern lifestyle does not allow to eliminate stress completely, but if can be reduced significantly with constant efforts. For example, if a positive thinking person or an optimist fails sometime, he does not blame himself for the same. He evaluates the genuine circumstances responsible for his failure and maintains a mindset of trying again. Optimistic people are more likely to succeed after failures.

On the other hand, if a pessimistic person fails, he straightaway blames his own caliber and looks down upon himself. He does not try to look at the circumstances responsible for his failure. They are reluctant to try the thing again after several negative experiences in life. It is already established by many researches that optimistic enjoy a better health and stronger relationships. They are much less stressful in their professional as well as personal life.

Positive thinking is a way of life, not just a project. You have to practice the positive way of thinking to make it your subconscious habit. If you become an optimist, you will see the negative events of life as just "flukes" and try to move ahead. And the positive events of your life will motivate you to enjoy your life even more.

For practicing optimism, you have to change only two things: self talk and public speaking. That is to say, whatever you talk to yourself should be positive and motivating. In addition, how you explain anything to the other person should also be positive. There is a huge difference between the talks of an optimist and a pessimist.

For instance, an optimist will respond to a new opportunity by saying, "It is a big opportunity to learn something new". On the other hand, a pessimist will respond to the same situation by saying, "I have never come across such a situation before". See the difference between the thought processes of the two and observe yourself who sounds better and feels good?

16. Meditation Helps

Meditation is a great method to show the exit door to stress. It is inexpensive and extremely effective. You can practice meditation anywhere and anytime. People around you would not even realize that you are meditating if you learn how to do it properly. Firstly, let us understand what is meditation? Then we will talk about how to do it.

Meditation is a combined medicine for mind and body. It takes you to a deep mode of relaxation. The tranquility of mind lets you eliminate the thoughts that keep occupying your mind. To meditate, you need to defocus your mind from all kinds of thoughts and focus all your attention to a single point in your head. The benefits of meditation are not limited to your session of meditation only.

Kinds of meditation

- When we say the word "Meditation", we are not sure about what it is. It actually covers a lot of aspects of relaxation. Many relaxation techniques and mediation types have some components of mediation. But, the goal of all techniques is only one-inner peace. Different ways of mediation are:

- **Guided meditation:** In this method, you have to visualize about any place that you find relaxing. You are required to use your maximum senses possible to reach the extreme level of visualization, viz. sight, smell, texture or sound. You may also take the help of a teacher or guide in this method.

- **Mantra meditation:** In this method, you need to constantly repeat a mantra or a calming word to achieve the state of inner peace.

- **Yoga:** Yoga is also a form of meditation, which requires you to focus on the movement of body rather than any other thoughts.

17.   Laughter is the Best Medicine

"Laughter is the best medicine" You must have heard that. It is used throughout the world to cure several chronic diseases. You do not need to visit a laughter therapist if you feel that there is no humor in your life. Laughter comes for free and you can easily indulge your body into it. Since your body cannot differentiate between fake laughter and genuine laughter, it just releases positive hormones when you are giggled. You can use laughter for stress management too. Let us see how:

Movies and TV: There is no dearth of comedy shows and movies. Just switch on the TV and watch any show you find funniest. You can also rent a DVD of your favorite childhood movie. You will roll out on the floor laughing.

Enjoy with friends: Laughter is contagious. You can go out with friends and watch a movie or just have a good time at your favorite restaurant. It is always good to share laughter with friends. Call them over for a night party and you can have a blast.

Find humor: It is easy to complain about the frustrations in life. Try laughing over them. There is no better remedy to laugh out loud over the problems of life. Even biggest of the issues seem trivial when you take them light heartedly.

"Fake it until you make it": Laughter therapy induces fake laughter only in the initial stages. You must have seen people deliberately laughing in groups in parks in the morning. They are practicing laughter only. Just by seeing others laughing, even the most depressed person cannot control himself and bursts into laughter. You can also try faking it until you achieve real merriment, which comes automatically in a while.

Chapter 7

Connect with Others

18.   Self-Compassion

Self-compassion means to extend kindness or compassion to oneself during the circumstances when one realizes one's inadequacy or failure. We all face such situations, when we realize our shortcomings. But, rather than indulging in self-criticism, we should be warm towards ourselves.

People who maintain high self- compassion cope in a better way with stress. Such people are open to their own suffering and get moved by it. They also reassure themselves when things go wrong. They maintain a non-judgmental attitude towards their inadequacies and recognize that their experience is just a part of common human experience. It means that they realize that they are not alone who are in problem. Humans are bound to suffer in one form or the other. This realization reduces the feeling of isolation in people and helps them to adapt to the hard times.

Another feature of self- compassion is to evaluate the circumstances in a balanced way and do not get carried away by the emotions. Self-compassionate people always handle the situations with mindfulness and cope with them in a better way. It does not mean that they are not emotional. Rather, they handle their emotions more maturely.

Just like optimism, self-compassion also comes with practice. You just need to adapt a more balanced outlook towards life. You should react to the negative as well as positive events in a balanced way. The balanced way of life is to take positive events more positively and take negative events less negatively.

19. Build Strong Relationships

Relationships are the pillars of life. People stay with you throughout your life in different forms of relationships. Whenever you face hard times, they support you. But, many a times it happens that you are left secluded when you are stressed. Thus, you have to help yourself to nurture and regain your relationships. Here, we will talk about how you can build strong relationships with people you already know.

Talk about common interests: Deepest of relationships start with small talk only. You must be having some friends who are more like acquaintances to you. Meet them and talk genuinely about yourself and listen to them too. You will find that you have discovered many things in common in just one meeting.

Express vulnerability: You and your friends know that you are not perfect. Still, you try to portray yourself as flawless. You need to do the opposite. When you express your vulnerabilities to them, you appear to be transparent with them and they want to talk with you even more. This is the first step of the ladder to build a strong relationship.

Have integrity: Whatever you say should be congruent to your actions. It makes you a person with high integrity in the eyes of the world and also keeps you stress free. If you do the opposite, you appear shallow in the eyes of your friends. Thus, you cannot make lifelong friendships with such way of life.

Be there in need: Your friends will come to you in hard times only when you seem reliable to them. You should also support them when they need you, not because you want their support in return; but because you as a friend should be dependable enough.

Establish Good Support System

Stress can be more powerfully dealt with, when you have a good social support system. A social support system helps in the following ways:

- When you vent your feelings to relatives and friends, you will start feeling better. Suppressed emotions are the leading cause for depression and bad moods. So you need to talk about the problems you face, share them with people you are close to, if you want to get effective stress relief.

- Social support helps in distracting you from the problem at hand, so you can find a better solution. Most often going over a problem continuously can make you confused and unable to arrive at a proper solution. With distractions such as going out with relatives or friends you will be able to free your mind, so you arrive at a better solution.

- Sharing the problem with others will mitigate the pain and make it easier to face the problem.

- A sound social support helps to heal depression quicker and the symptoms become less severe.

- Sharing a problem with an intelligent relative or friend can help you find a permanent solution for your problem.

Conclusion

Stress is undoubtedly a part of our life whether we want it or not. However, at the same time it is not right to be stressed out continuously. You need to understand that you need not have to control whatever happens in your life.

Reacting in a distraught, overwhelmed, or frazzled way to a challenging or difficult situation is not the right way to deal with it. The higher our stress levels the more we are prone to risk of flu, colds, and even life threatening illnesses.

Moreover, we would not enjoy the bounties that life showers on us. For your emotional and physical benefit, knowing how to manage stress will help immensely. Reading this book would have helped you know about the ill effects of stress and the ways by which you can successfully be free of the life shattering stress permanently. The various tips elaborated are proven relief measures that are sure to get you out of the stress rut you are in. Best of luck!

www.ingramcontent.com/pod-product-compliance
Lightning Source LLC
Chambersburg PA
CBHW050834290526
45792CB00001B/395